The Brothellian Manifesto

Grayson | Silverman

'I will cut myself a path through the world or perish in the attempt. Others have begun life with nothing and ended Greatly. And shall I remain idle? No, I will carve myself the passage to Grandeur, but never with Dishonour'

Lord Byron

'Life is not long enough to drivel through a bad fashion and begin again'

William Holman Hunt

Preface

1. Welcome to the Brothellian Movement, a provocative alliance of artists, writers, poets and performers joined together by one common goal — to ignite the fires of a new cultural renaissance. It is a movement that is broad in its appeal yet rich in talent, attracting ever greater numbers of artists and intellectuals to its rank each day. Like us, they are contemptuous of the status quo in the world of art & literature. They are discontented with the dominance of post-modern ideals that consistently fail to connect with the majority of people and serve only to indulge the incestuous fetishes of an artistic elite. They are dissatisfied with the lack of value attached to expert craftsmanship and genuine talent in the arts — features that ought to be so integral to our creative output. And they are disgusted with the mindless pursuit of fame and the celebrity culture which accommodates it, a culture which has infected art & literature, leading to a situation where an artist's name is held in higher esteem than the actual work of art itself. When people look back at our culture two hundred years from now, do we want them to uncover an age of cultural abandon, or do we want them to unearth a bounty of literary and artistic treasures that can withstand the tempests of trend and time?

2. The Brothellian Movement is the alternative to the status quo — a new breed of visionaries who have developed a unique and sexually compelling way to celebrate art & literature. It is our belief that these individuals will come to define the essence of what it means to be a working artist and, in doing so, spark a cultural renaissance that will reignite our desire to produce the rich and imaginative art of which future generations will be proud.

3. This belief is reaffirmed each day as more talented individuals make a commitment to the guiding principles of Brothellian Ideology, putting its ideas into practice in ever more imaginative ways. They are attracted by the ambition of the movement and the seductive way in which we present our work. Indeed, it is this commitment to inspiring our audiences that is one of the key hallmarks of the Brothellian individual. We want people to be so

excited by our work that they actually *want* to invest in us, rather than feeling obliged to; we want them to feel so captivated by the enduring charm of art & literature that they enjoy making repeat business in our ventures.

4. Another key hallmark is the potent combination of determination and integrity. We are single-minded in the belief that all creative endeavours should be underpinned by a commitment to the tenets of craftsmanship, talent and imagination, but we are also non-prescriptive in terms of the artistic journey and individual style of any particular artist or collective. Anything less would be to undermine our deep respect for artistic freedom.

5. The words in this document set out the guiding principles of the Brothellian agenda. They are intended to inspire like-minded artists and performers to develop their own unique ways of disseminating their art in an enticing and imaginative manner. In doing so, we are connecting a wider community of visionaries who are committed to restoring the pivotal role of art & literature in society. Ultimately, we envisage that these Brothellian principles will permeate every artistic discipline in a new age of cultural enrichment, where proactivity and timeless quality is celebrated by all. By joining the Brothellian Movement, you can help lead this change.

0. Introduction: The Brothellian agenda

0.1. What it means to be 'Brothellian': definitions and origin

6. We are often asked why we have chosen to adopt the image and ideas of historical Brothels in our movement for a culturally-enriched society. Let us first be clear that our appropriation of "The Brothel" is not merely for aesthetic value. Rather, it stems from a deep-seated affinity we have with the instincts and ambitions of the Brothel owner – namely, a desire to feed our audience's innermost cravings in the most seductive way possible, appealing to their primal needs. We believe that this applies as much to cultural fulfilment as it does to sexual fulfilment, which is why any event which bears the Brothellian hallmark is always characterised by an alluring mix of well-crafted talent and enticing imagery. We want people to be so stimulated by what they see and hear that they feel compelled to invest in the tantalising delights on offer, receiving much pleasure from doing so. This is the foundation of Brothellian thinking and the cornerstone of the Brothellian approach to promoting and valuing artistic talent.

0.2 Outlining the Brothellian agenda

7. Of course, there is evidence of Brothellian thinking throughout history and many examples can be drawn of individuals or collectives displaying Brothellian *tendencies* – for example, the bold and dramatic life of Lord Byron, which challenged the typically conservative image of a poet's role in society; or the crude illustrations of Beardsley which often mocked or conflicted with Victorian sensibility. What marks the Brothellian Movement as distinct, however, is the coming together of a wide range of artists and performers – across all different disciplines – under a common set of principles that represent the Brothellian agenda. So although Brothellian tendencies have existed in the minds of many people previously, it is only recently that it has come to be defined as a movement in itself.

8. Furthermore, it is a movement that has grown out of necessity and not out of the minds of a self-proclaimed artistic elite. There has never been another

point in history where so many artists and audiences have felt so detached from the prevailing culture and the values associated with it. The pre-eminence of conceptual art, allied with a rising neglect of expert craftsmanship, has left many people feeling that our culture is at best 'a joke' and at worst 'an artistic travesty'. Alongside this is a mainstream obsession with vacuous celebrity and instantaneous fame, values which are seemingly at odds with the Brothellian commitment to investing in talent and achieving mastery in our craft.

9. The prevailing culture brings with it the danger of alienating a whole generation and of failing to recognise a wealth of talented artists and performers. It is no wonder that so many people – artists and audiences – have been attracted by the alternative provided by the Brothellian Movement. Rather then alienating people, the Brothellian instinct is to entice them by utilising the sex appeal of talent and presenting our work in an irresistible way. In place of elitist art and celebrity culture, we will always seek to promote talent and respect the intelligence of our audiences – indeed, one of the great Brothellian instincts is to always look for the highest common denominator, taking people along in the pursuit of artistic excellence.

0.3 Promoting the Brothellian agenda: principles for cultural enrichment

10. This manifesto contains a set of guiding principles for the Brothellian individual to follow. They are non-prescriptive in nature, derived as they are from the thoughts and actions of many artists and intellectuals working tirelessly to promote a richer and more stimulating culture. These principles have been brought together in order to identify a clear Brothellian agenda in art & literature. They are intended to inspire rather than instruct, a foundation on which like-minded individuals can ignite the fires of a new cultural renaissance.

1. Valuing our Artistic Communities

1.1 The problem with 'freebies'

11. The first principle of the Brothellian Movement is that creative talent should always be valued and nurtured. There is a real danger in providing our abilities free of charge, and emerging artists and performers are all too often dragged into this quagmire. This is completely understandable – we all want to advance in our respective fields and build the networks that will bring us success in the future. However, the over-exposure of free art and entertainment creates an expectation in the audience's mind that this is the prevailing order and perhaps an assumption that the work itself is of little or no value (whether this decision is made consciously or not). This kind of environment breeds disaster; not only does it increase the likelihood of a talented artist feeling worthless or undervalued, it also encourages a lack of quality control in our creative endeavors.

12. In reality, we know such endeavours carry substantial economic value, whether this is measured in terms of an artist's input or by the benefit to society from cultural activity. This needs to be reflected in the value we attach to all forms of creative output, based not on the artist's status but on the timeless quality of work produced. Across many artistic disciplines, there is a general acceptance that an artist's worth is only truly recognised when they have achieved a certain level of fame; such is the predominance of celebrity culture in Western civilisation. It is a worrying trend when an artist's name is valued above the work of art itself.

1.2 A Brothellian Approach to valuing art

13. In contrast, the Brothellian instinct is to value all works of art, regardless of an individual's status, so long as they display an enduring commitment to the tenets of craftsmanship, talent and imagination. Moreover, the success of Brothellian events staged around the globe proves that most people share our understanding of the value of art. The Poetry Brothel is a great example of this, attracting a diverse and non-traditional poetry audience and

stimulating them enough to make them want to invest in the seductive verse of their 'whores'.

14. The success of the Brothellian approach rests on a combination of exciting the audience whilst staying firm in our commitment to artistic integrity. It is an approach that is constantly evolving and being adapted to suit the promotion of many different art forms, including life drawing, illustration, burlesque and photography, to name but a few. The more this approach evolves, the closer we will move towards recognising the true value of art's role in society.

1.3 Appreciating our audience: the flipside of valuing our artistic communities

15. The role of the audience is pivotal in our approach as it is they who will ultimately see the value in our art. Brothellian individuals never underestimate the intelligence of their audience, nor do they seek to win favour by courting the lowest common denominator. The market is saturated with enough intellectually-vacuous material already – let's not add to it! Indeed, our experience from staging Brothellian events has shown that audiences agree with this sentiment. Also, we share their widespread scepticism over the contrived nature (whether real or perceived) of much post-modernism and conceptualism within contemporary art. Brothellian artists believe it is better to be open and honest with audiences, to invite them into our imaginations and share with them the passion we've invested in developing our talent and mastering our craft.

2. Presenting our Work in an Irresistible Way

2.1. Taking art & literature to the people

16. Of course, an audience is not a 'fixed' concept. It can be directly influenced in the way we reach out to people, enticing them with the seductive appeal of our talents. Society is busy, and we believe that the best way to bring our creative endeavours to a wider audience is by taking it into the heart of their communities, so that people can access it with relative ease and feel comfortable in the surroundings in which it is provided. So, for example, an illustrator with Brothellian tendencies may decide to sell his services in the environment of a local public house; similarly, a group of performers might stage a decadent soirée in the nightclubbing district of a major city on a busy Saturday night. This approach is driven by the desire to make art & literature easy to access and shameless to receive – again, following the instincts and ambitions of the Brothel owner.

2.2. Extending creativity to presentation as well as content

17. The other way to attract a wider audience is to create intriguing atmosphere around all endeavours, capturing people's imagination in the way we present ourselves and our work. In order to stand out from the crowd, we need to apply the same creativity in promoting and selling our work as we do in actually making it. In a visual sense, we need to be conspicuous in the environment in which we operate in, either by enhancing the image we present of ourselves or by taking our work to unusual environments where one wouldn't usually expect to find such talent. It is this idea of 'standing out from the crowd' and being bold in our pro-activity that creates the aura to draw in an audience.

2. 3. Having the greatest visual impact

18. The aesthetics we choose to adopt are centred on having the greatest visual impact to complement our work. We always aim to be visually striking in our appearance, selecting the outfits, furnishings and ornaments that will enhance the multisensory experience of our shows. Brothellian events are

known for creating an atmosphere of intrigue and seductiveness, features that distinguish us from the banality of routine and the comfort of mass-produced culture.

19. Having glorious aesthetics is not just of benefit to the audience, but to the artist as well. A suitably adorned environment can ascend work to attain pertinent meaning and higher presence. It can also enable a stronger connection with the essence of art, raising the intensity of performance or spectacle to a severely profound level, such is the *power* of aesthetics, but it cannot tranform works of mediocrity above that of mediocrity.

20. Of course, Brothellian individuals will often take part in events that do not bear the Brothellian hallmark or have any Brothellian tendencies – in fact, we actively encourage them to do so. However, this is not an invitation to abandon our principles; rather it is an opportunity to apply them in ever more imaginative ways, being creative and flexible in how we interpret them. In terms of aesthetics, this may mean adopting an outward appearance that is seemingly at odds with the event itself, sparking a culture clash which heightens the levels of drama and intensity. There is always scope to apply Brothellian thinking, whether we choose to complement or contrast with our environments, but it must always be done with a view to maximising our visual impact and the artistic experience.

21. In the English branch of the Brothellian movement, there has been a conscious decision to blend the aesthetics of Byronic exoticism with Brothels from the Victorian era in our events. This has enabled artists and performers to draw upon the unique and illustrious heritage of our country within their own artistic craft. Moreover, it complements the alluring nature of our ideals and the enduring relevance of the Brothellian vision. However, were we to actually exist in such periods, we would have to stage a very different type of event in order to stand out and be visually striking. Ultimately, it is a matter of context and impact, creating the aesthetic environment that is most suitable to promoting our art and ambition. This is essential to showcase the sex appeal of talent.

2.4. The 'Sex Appeal' of talent

22. Brothellian individuals understand that our creative talents and imagination are sexually intriguing, and that this holds great mystery to others. There is no shame in 'sexing up' the arts as the appeal is already there, it's just rarely commented upon. Only in rock music have artists regularly been harnessing the sex appeal of talent over the most recent decades; we believe the time is ripe to apply the same knowledge to other artistic fields. Ultimately, we envisage a society where the quill or the sketchbook holds as much sexual potency as the electric guitar; where the illustrator or poet is as much of a sex symbol as the rock star. Indeed, in the Romantic era, the poet often carried great sexual appeal; the fact that this has been lost in contemporary poetry owes much to the ascendancy of desperate earnestness and sycophancy which has spread across the discipline like the plague. Fortunately, Poetry Brothels are addressing this imbalance; the knowledge gained from such ventures is now being applied to other aspects of the arts so they too can realise their inherent appeal and seductive intent.

23. As much as celebrity culture can excite, so too can the sex appeal of talent. The difference is that Brothellian individuals value ability and investment in art, whereas the prevailing culture has been distorted by an over-emphasis on celebrity and vacuous entertainment. By promoting the sex appeal of talent, we can build a much richer culture, based upon an appreciation of artistic talents and their alluring nature.

3. The Imperative of Human Contact

3.1. Maintaining humanity in the digital age

24. We live in the digital age; of that there is no question. Any artist, writer or performer with aspirations above the mediocre must maintain an online presence and stay at the edge of developments in digital and media technology. However, as more and more human activity shifts online – in everything from social interaction to purchasing consumer products – there is an even greater need for the physical activities that maintain our shared sense of humanity. Brothellian individuals stand at the forefront of this change, being able to provide one of the few arenas where human interaction can substantially enhance the viewer's experience, on both a spiritual and emotional level. A painting by Caravaggio may look impressive on a computer screen, but when you witness the delicate brush strokes of his vivid imagination first hand, knowing that he stood before the very canvas you are now viewing, it becomes a transcendental experience that deepens our understanding of the human condition.

25. The rapid advance of digital technology should not be seen as a threat but as a great opportunity for artists and performers. We can provide people with the art, entertainment and spiritual revelations that will sustain our sense of a shared humanity as we move through the digital age. Experience proves that this is what people want. Witness, for example, the coming together of people at street parties across Britain in celebration of Royal Weddings and Coronations; or the 'sing along' moments at music festivals where all kinds of people join together in a song's simple refrain which captures a collective experience. All Brothellian individuals are driven by the desire to maintain humanity in the digital age through our showcases and events, recognising the glorious attraction of physical interaction in the same way Brothel owners have always done.

3.2. The Culture of Events: the necessity of human interaction

26. Indeed, there is real insight to be gained from that moment of connection

between artist and audience. This is something that is much more difficult, albeit not impossible, to capture online. The instant feedback and shared sense of humanity from a live event allows an artist to develop a better understanding of their own work and how best to present it to a myriad of audiences.

27. At Brothellian events, the artist or performer derives an even greater advantage due to the diverse and atypical audiences the movement attracts. Because of the unusual and alluring places in which we stage our events, we are able to entice multiple cross-sections of society which traditional arts events and elitist institutions consistently fail to connect with. For instance, at a typical Brothellian event – perhaps an oxymoron in itself – an artist or performer may gain the chance to parade their talents in front of a couple of corporate bankers, some employees from a local fast-food chain, and a leading theatre director, all in quick succession (this example is taken from our own personal experience). This welcoming, seductive and non-elitist attitude sets the Brothellian Movement apart from any other cultural phenomena.

4. Fearless in our Proactive Attitude

4.1. How to dominate and control barriers

28. One of the key hallmarks of the Brothellian individual is the potent combination of determination and integrity. This is demonstrated by the fearless approach we take in defining our art and the proactive attitude in which we champion our ideals. This determination is essential to convincing others of the value of talent and the strength of one's beliefs, for with belief comes a dedication to lifelong investment in developing one's craft to such a point where it becomes an elite skill, yet never with the elitist attitude that infects many contemporary arts establishments.

29. This staunch dedication – based on the twin attributes of determination and integrity – is essential in realising the true value of our art. When aligned with a flexible imagination to problem-solving, it can hold the key to understanding how to dominate and control barriers. Artists, writers and performers who don't yet possess these skills often perceive such barriers as insurmountable obstacles to their development; however, those with sharpened vision and resilience see them as pivotal challenges which force us of our comfort zone, encouraging greater flexibility and variation in our approach to art.

30. Moreover, barriers can actually aid our creativity and propel our artistic development in unexpected and innovative directions. If necessity is the mother of invention, then it is also the playground of an imaginative spirit. For instance, if a fashion designer is unable to grasp the predominant style of a particular season, they should instead develop their own unique style that challenges the mainstream thought process. If a painter is finding limited opportunities to display their work, they should set about creating their own exhibition space – one that complements their work in a visually striking way. This approach rests on a deep understanding of the positive role that barriers play and our unique ability to dominate and control them as Brothellian individuals and collectives.

4.2. Creating alternatives to the institutional orthodoxy

31. One of the main barriers emerging artists face when promoting their work is an institutional orthodoxy that is unbending in its adoption of new ideas or challenging perceptives. It is all too often the case that the prevailing culture distances itself from radical artists, only to embrace them when they have become publicly acceptable and commercially successful. The Brothellian Movement is contemptuous of this perverted orthodoxy and is weary of those who seek to appeal to it. We believe that such attitudes are short-sighted in nature and run contrary to our agenda of igniting a culturally-enriched society.

32. By creating our own avenues for expression, Brothellian artists ensure that they stay true to their artistic integrity and don't feel the need to cower for the whims and fancies of cultural leaders or government funding bodies. It allows us to create the aesthetic platforms that complement our work and attract an audience that reaches beyond the conventional. This is the essence of an inclusive, liberated culture.

33. We have the opportunity to take charge of our cultural direction and create ever more imaginative ways of attracting audiences to invest in us. Brothellian individuals are able to define their own artistic style and cultivate their own following, not feeling the need to 'tap into' an already established audience. In this way, it bears close similarities to the Punk ethic of 'do it yourself'. By adopting this fearless and proactive attitude, we can re-define the essence of creativity and value in our artistic fields and contribute to a more enticing, vibrant and imaginative culture that everyone can be proud of.

5. Never Compromising our Artistic Integrity

5.1. Seeking truth in content

34. So far, little has been mentioned of the type of content or specific styles employed by Brothellian artists. This has been intentional, allowing the focus of the manifesto to fall upon the imaginative ways in which we can promote the value of art and attract wider audiences to our events. We know that great works of art continue to be created but they are all too often lost in the celebrity-driven, post-modern blandness which dominates and obscures our cultural landscape. Our mission is to help talented artists gain the pre-eminence they deserve, not to tell them how they should be making their art.

35. To be prescriptive in terms of content would run in direct contrast to Brothellian ideals. We believe that artistic talent has to be free in order to flourish, a belief which precludes any temptation to define the precise features that great art & literature should consist of. Only a commitment to the tenets of craftsmanship, talent and imagination are necessary for the Brothellian artist to prosper. Indeed, a prescriptive approach may inhibit the individual or collective imagination and potentially harm the quest for artistic excellence. In addition, it would actually eliminate one of most attractive elements of our work, its integrity, which adds much to the sex appeal of talent and sustains the intrigue of Brothellian art. There may be certain practical constraints which hinder an individual from having complete control over their work, but this should not discourage them from bringing personal flavour to the table. There's very little appealing in that which is contrived and bends over backwards to accommodate the tastes and whims of a specific audience, at least in the long-term.

5.2. Respecting the intellectual capacity of our audiences

36. The Brothellian Movement is centred on the desire to attract and entice audiences, but it is not about compromising on content or trying desperately to appease the people who come to our events, shows and exhibitions, (to do so would be to undermine the intellectual capacity of our audience and to

devalue our artistic integrity). It is the Brothellian instinct to always appeal to the highest common denominator; to never settle for mediocrity or benign success.

37. Of course, the highest common denominator is always evolving; such is the human appetite for new ideas and fresh perceptions of beauty. One of the great challenges for any Brothellian individual is trying to capture the highest common denominator as it constantly changes and evolves. To understand that audiences evolve and adapt in the same way artists do is essential is realising the transformative potential of the Brothellian agenda and our ability to provoke change.

6. Conclusion: Setting out the Brothellian Vision

38. The wheels of the Brothellian agenda are firmly in motion and the movement is progressing at an accelerating pace. For too long, our society has been saturated by a vacuous celebrity culture and a post-modern approach to art that is contrived and essentially elitist. Indeed, these corrupt forces have come to define our cultural output in the first decade of the twenty first century; let's make sure they never hold the same status again.

39. For beneath the superficiality of the mainstream, there is a wealth of artistic talent and enterprising individuals who deserve to have their value recognised; waves of people who are wholly committed to achieving artistic excellence through their craft, talent and imaginations. Many of these artists are excited by the ideology of the Brothellian Movement, sharing the desire to have the true value of art appreciated and recognised. The guiding principles of the movement offer a framework by which like-minded individuals and collectives can set about forming their own innovative ways of attracting audiences and enthralling them with their unique abilities and masterful creativity. In doing so, we can contribute to a more vibrant, alluring and inclusive culture that has the capacity and integrity to overpower the dominance of post-modernist society.

40. We urge all who hear this to be fearless and daring in starting their own ventures, taking inspiration from the principles outlined in this manifesto. Indeed, the principles themselves have been based upon the practical actions and initiatives developed by artists and performers within the Brothellian Movement. As with the movement itself, the core ideas are constantly evolving and adapting as they are brought to new environments with their own distinct cultures and historical influences. The interaction between these elements - i.e. the principles, the artists and the environments - has sparked a rich and dynamic movement that has a wealth of talent behind it, ready to drive the Brothellian vision into new and exciting territories.

41. Together, we can ignite and inspire a new cultural renaissance that both artists and audiences can take pride in: a culture based upon Brothellian

principles and the imaginative capacity of the people who enact them; which always endorses the value of craftsmanship, talent and imagination in art & literature; that reaches out to greater audiences by presenting our work in a seductive and captivating way; a culture that realises the importance of human interaction in the digital age and the unique opportunities it brings; that is courageous in starting up new ventures and avenues for talented artists and performers to express themselves; and that always respects the intelligence of our audiences and shares their aspiration for a richer and more exciting culture. This is the Brothellian vision; welcome to Brothelliana.

www.ingramcontent.com/pod-product-compliance
Lightning Source LLC
Chambersburg PA
CBHW051227170526
45166CB00005B/2069